MW00639037

THEY DIED TOO YOUNG

SERGEI GRINKOV

Anne E. Hill

CHELSEA HOUSE PUBLISHERS
Philadelphia

The Chelsea House World Wide Web address is
http://www.chelseahouse.com

Printed and bound in The Hashemite Kingdom of Jordan.
First Printing
1 3 5 7 9 8 6 4 2

Cover photo: Sergei Grinkov (AP Photo)

Library of Congress Cataloging-in-Publication Data
Hill, Anne E., 1974–
    Sergei Grinkov / Anne E. Hill.
        p. cm. — (They died too young.)
    Includes bibliographical references (p.).
    Summary: Presents a biography of the Russian pairs skater who
died in 1995 at the age of twenty-eight from a heart attack. Focuses
on his life with skating partner and wife, Ekaterina Gordeeva.
    ISBN 0-7910-5855-7
    1. Grinkov, Sergei, 1967–1995—Biography—Juvenile literature.
2. Skaters—Russia (Federation)—Juvenile literature. [1. Grinkov,
Sergei, 1967–1995. 2. Ice skaters. 3. Gordeeva, Ekaterina.]
I. Title. II. Series.
GV850.G67 H57 2000
796.91'2'092—dc21
    [B]   00-026947
                                                   CIP

Picture Credits: AP Photo: pp. 4, 9, 29, 35, 38, 40, 44, 45, 46; Corbis:
pp. 16, 24, 32; Corel: p. 10

Publishing Coordinator Jim McAvoy
Editorial Assistant Rob Quinn
Contributing Editor Amy Handy

Acknowledgments
Thanks to Sylvia Yu of the G&G International Fan Club,
Deb Nast, and Ekaterina Gordeeva.

*For George
I cherish every day with you.*

ABOUT THE AUTHOR
Anne E. Hill has written six books for Chelsea House, including
Denzel Washington, which was named one of the New York Public
Library's Best Books for Teenagers; *Ekaterina Gordeeva; Female
Firsts in Their Fields: Broadcasting and Journalism; Cameron Diaz;*
and *Jennifer Lopez.* Mrs. Hill is also a writer for the Concert
Connections' All-Stars Teen Hotline. A long-time admirer of
Gordeeva and Grinkov, she writes from her home in Wayne,
Pennsylvania, where she lives with her husband, George.

CONTENTS

Ekaterina Gordeeva and Sergei Grinkov skate their way to
a gold medal during the pairs free skating competition at
Hamar Olympic Amphitheatre in Hamar, Norway.

PERFECTION ON ICE

The lights went up in the Olympic skating center in Lillehammer, Norway, and the crowd was roaring. Yet despite the enthusiastic applause, 26-year-old Sergei Grinkov was disappointed with his performance. He and his wife and pairs skating partner, Ekaterina Gordeeva—or Katia, as she is known—were considered perhaps the best in the sport and favored to medal at these 1994 winter Games. Sergei was usually dependable in competition, rarely missing a jump or a lift. But he had just singled a double jump, and his usually clean spins were out of sync with Katia's.

Breathless, he left the ice and waited for the inevitable news that they had lost the gold medal. Sergei was prepared for the disappointment and determined not to feel too unhappy. After all, he and Katia had already won one gold medal at the 1988 Games, and just a year earlier, the two had thought they would never compete in another Olympics.

In 1993, Katia and Sergei were the parents of a one-year-old baby girl, Daria, and making a good living as professional pairs skaters. They enjoyed touring the world with each other and doing what they loved. While they longed for the thrill of another Olympic Games, the International Skating Union (ISU) forbid professionals from competing. However, after letters from several professional skaters and much deliberation, the ISU changed its rules. It decided that professionals could write to the ISU and request that their amateur status be reinstated. If they made it through the difficult qualifiers, just like all the other amateurs, to reach the Games, they could compete. Katia and Sergei decided to do just that.

5

They gave up their financial security and moved Daria and Katia's mother, Elena, with them to Ottawa, Canada, to train with their favorite choreographer, Marina Zueva. Marina had been planning a special artistic program for the pair for years and she knew that now was the time to use it. Skaters in the Olympics perform two programs: a short technical program, which requires pairs skaters to demonstrate certain jumps, lifts, and throws, and a longer artistic program, with as many unique elements as they choose. Marina knew that the music of Beethoven's "Moonlight Sonata" was the perfect tone for the artistic program. She also knew that the theme of man celebrating woman as the mother of all mankind was just right for the romance of Sergei and Katia, especially since they were now parents. Sergei loved the music more than any other they had skated to in their 12-year career together. For their short program, Katia, Sergei, and Marina decided on Spanish gypsy-style dance music known as flamenco. They set to work creating their routines and training.

Despite the fact that Sergei and Katia were in great physical shape, they still put in long hours of on- and off-ice conditioning. In addition to skating, they took ballet classes, ran, lifted weights, and played tennis to increase their coordination. The pair took their workouts very seriously because they knew that while they were experienced skaters, there were many young skaters who had been training long and hard for this opportunity. The drive and strength of their competitors were always in the back of their minds.

Marina, however, knew that their skating had improved since their last Olympic win. Since the 1988 Games, they had fallen in love, married, and had a baby. Their closeness made them more like one on the ice. "You're doing everything I told you so perfectly. It's almost like you were preparing your whole career for this program," Marina told them one day.

Sergei felt that way as well; he identified with the piece and loved to skate it. In the beginning of the program, he is on his knees before Katia. Then they open their arms to the judges before proceeding to "tell" the story of their lives. The music helped them tell this story, because, as Katia said, "It expresses what changes love can bring about in people, how it can make them stronger, make them have more respect for each other. How it can give them the ability to bring a new life into the world."

Once their routines were established, the family moved back to their native Russia for more training and costume fittings. Their costumer, Vladislav Kostin, picked simple navy blue velvet outfits with a white stripe down the front and around the collar. As soon as their costumes were ready, it was fall—time for pre-Olympic competitions. The pair won Skate Canada and the Russian Nationals, which qualified them for the Olympics. Another win at the European Championships in early 1994 gave the pair even more confidence. But these first-place finishes did not diminish Sergei's drive to keep training for the Games. He and Katia woke up early to work on each individual element of their programs. One day they focused on spins, the next day on jumps, then choreography, until there was nothing more for them to perfect.

But Katia felt that there was one more thing they needed to do. Before they traveled to Norway, the pair visited Father Nikolai, the Russian Orthodox priest who had married them almost three years earlier. Although Katia was close with the priest and visited him before each competition, Sergei had never gone with her. The two had been so focused on their goal that hearing the priest's inspiring words reminded them that winning the medal should not consume them. "I can't pray for you to win," he said. "You have to look for each other for this. You can't ask God to please help you win. Better to ask that He give you the chance to be happy when you skate. And remember your Daria, that you're skating for her."

Sergei recalled Father Nikolai's words when they arrived in the Olympic village and settled in. He held a nervous Katia's hand, and they got ready for competition together.

Many young skaters resented their return to the amateur ranks, but Katia and Sergei ignored their negative comments. The media also questioned why they had returned. Sergei did not speak English very well, so he didn't answer the questions. More news people were at these Games than any other. Just weeks earlier, singles skater Nancy Kerrigan had been hit on the knee with a piece of pipe. The assault almost took her out of competition and brought a lot of attention to the skating world. Later the attacker was linked to a fellow Olympic hopeful, skater Tonya Harding. Sergei and Katia were saddened by the event, but couldn't think about it too much—the pairs skaters were first to perform.

Despite finishing ahead of the music in their short program, Gordeeva and Grinkov were in the lead, with another Russian pair, Natalia Mishkutenok and Artur Dmitriev, in second place. While they were in a good position to win their second gold, Sergei was worried. He didn't sleep well the night before the long program, and he had no appetite the next day. But he didn't want to worry Katia, so he kept his nervousness to himself.

As the two took to the ice, Katia thought he looked as strong and calm as always. But after the routine, she knew something was wrong. "I asked him simply. 'Double?' He shook his head. It was the first mistake I could remember him ever making. He was very upset, but unless you knew him well, you wouldn't have known," she revealed.

The two closest pairs of competitors—Canadian pair Isabelle Brasseur and Lloyd Eisler and Mishkutenok and Dmitriev—had skated their artistic programs perfectly before Katia and Sergei took the ice. Natalia and Artur, who was a good friend of Sergei's, had even received a standing ovation for their performance. The pressure was on Gordeeva and Grinkov.

Moments later, Sergei and Katia stood on the medals podium as the Russian national anthem played. Despite Sergei's mistake, eight of nine judges had scored them first,

Russian gold medalists Gordeeva and Grinkov (center) stand proudly on the podium at the 1994 winter Olympics.

and they won the gold medal. Their routine was inspired, and everyone loved it. The pair accepted colorful bouquets of tulips and waved to the cheering crowd. But Sergei was still unhappy. "Gold medal or not, " Katia said, "he was not used to making mistakes." While his friends on the speed skating team got him to crack a smile as he accepted his medal, Sergei believed this would not be his last Olympic Games. He and Katia had won this gold medal for each other, but it was flawed with the memory of his mistake. "He wanted to skate in the Nagano Olympics in 1998," Katia remembered. "He wanted to compete again, to erase that single blemish from his thoughts. He kept this wish inside him for over a year before mentioning it to me. A third Olympic bid. I didn't think I could handle the pressure of another Olympics, but I couldn't say no, because I saw the hope in his eyes."

From the beginning, Sergei Grinkov was determined— a perfectionist with tremendous athletic ability and a love for skating.

An evening view of Moscow, Russia.

LIFE IN MOSCOW

Sergei Mikhailovich Grinkov was born on February 4, 1967, in Moscow, the capital of the then Union of Soviet Socialist Republics (U.S.S.R.). Russians do not have original middle names. Instead, they are given a birth name, followed by variations of their father's first and last names. Sergei's middle name was derived from the first name of his father, Mikhail Kondrateyevich Grinkov. When Daria was born 25 years later, she became Daria Sergeyevna Grinkova.

Mikhail and his wife, Anna Filipovna Grinkova, both worked for the Moscow Police Department. When Sergei was born they already had a seven-year-old daughter, Natalia Mikhailovna Grinkov. Despite the age difference between them, Sergei and Natalia were very close, and because both of their parents worked long hours, Natalia was often left to care for her little brother.

The Grinkov family was originally from the city of Lipetsk, which is about an eight-hour train ride from Moscow. In many Russian families, the grandparents care for their grandchildren when the parents go to work. But because Sergei's grandparents were so far away and Natalia was in school, young Sergei was often left at an overnight center for children. Anna and Mikhail would drop off their towheaded son on Monday morning and not return to pick him up until Friday afternoon. "Sometimes his parents told him, 'Don't worry, Sergei, we'll be back to pick you up early, maybe on Wednesday or Thursday,'" Katia later wrote in her memoir, *My Sergei*. "He'd wait and wait, his little face peering out a window at the street, and when they didn't keep their word, he'd cry."

One winter, Sergei's parents sent him to a camp where the children took their naps outside in hammocks in the cold, snowy weather. The children who didn't cry got a piece of chocolate. Sergei was often a recipient of this treat, because at a very young age he had learned how to be tough and keep his disappointment to himself. While the condition of Sergei's care may seem almost like abuse to many, it was not unusual for children in the U.S.S.R.

From 1945 until 1991, the U.S.S.R. was one of the world's two "superpowers." The other was the United States, with whom the U.S.S.R. shared strained relations. The country was ruled by Communism, a central bureaucracy that regulated the people of the Soviet Union. Under this regime, Russians were not allowed to own property. The state controlled everything from the amount of food on store shelves to the manufacturing of cars and home appliances. The goal of the Communist Party was to create a society that provided equally for the needs of all its citizens.

Unfortunately, the ideals of Communism were never realized in the Soviet Union. For many, life was similar to that in a Third World country. There wasn't enough housing, there was little fresh food on store shelves, and there were too many shoddy products. Prior to the collapse of Communism in 1991, citizens of the U.S.S.R. were troubled and unhappy with their government. Even now, they struggle to rid themselves of the internal problems created by Communism.

One way to have a better life during these hard years was to be a successful athlete. These athletes were not treated as other citizens were, as originally intended under Communism. Sports stars were revered in the U.S.S.R. and often given money, cars, homes, and many other luxuries not afforded to the average citizen.

At a young age, Sergei knew he wanted to be an athlete. He liked a variety of sports, including swimming, tennis, soccer, and hockey. Sergei had natural athletic ability, and at just five years old, was accepted into the Central Red Army

School (the Russian acronym for the club was CSKA). There, students took regular classes in addition to training for their respective sports.

Early on at CSKA, Sergei was chosen to train as a skater. He was small and strong, two good qualities for skating, which was a popular new sport in the 1970s. Young Sergei showed great promise as a singles skater. Every day he wore his school uniform, a navy blue jacket and pants. But as soon as young Sergei was dressed, he was dirty. "[His mother would] change him for school, warn him not to get dirty, and the next thing she knew, Sergei would have fallen into a tub of water," Katia joked.

Sergei's tendency to get dirty may have been an accident, or perhaps it was a show of rebellion. The youngster hated conformity and often liked to liven up his uniform to stand out from the crowd. When a teenage Sergei caught young Katia Gordeeva's eye, he wasn't wearing the mandatory uniform, but slacks, a jacket, and a skinny leather tie. He liked to be stylish and carried a briefcase, rather than a shoulder bag like his friends.

At CSKA, Sergei was a successful skater, but he struggled with his jumps. Still, he performed three triple jumps in competition in Budapest, Hungary, when he was not yet 14. In the summer of 1981, Sergei was surprised when the school officials decided he should become a pairs skater. The seventh grader was unsure of having a partner. He was also doubtful if he was strong enough to lift someone while skating. But the school thought differently; they had their eye on another young skater whom they thought would make a good match for Grinkov.

Ten-year-old Ekaterina was a tiny, serious skater who also showed promise. But, like Sergei, her jumps were weak. When she learned she was going to be paired with the older, stylish Sergei, Katia was both excited and scared. "I had never spoken to him. I remembered seeing him on the ice with the older boys, and also in school, and he was slender and narrow and handsome," Katia remembered. "But Sergei was so much older than me—four years, which at that age seems like a lifetime."

The two new partners also found that they had very different personalities and backgrounds. Katia was born on May 28, 1971, to Alexander Alexeyevich Gordeev and Elena Levovna Gordeeva. She was the oldest child in the family, with a little sister, Maria, who was born when Katia was three. While both of Katia's parents worked (Katia's father was a folk dancer and her mother was a teletype operator for a Soviet news agency), her grandparents lived in the family's three-bedroom apartment. Katia's grandmother, whom she and Maria lovingly called "babushka," cared for the girls, and they grew up happy and loved. Katia seemed oblivious to the pain that many people in the U.S.S.R. were experiencing. Because her grandfather had been a colonel in the tank division during World War II, the Gordeevs were deemed important to the Soviet Union and given special privileges, much like athletes.

Despite her idyllic life, Katia wasn't as lively as Sergei. She followed the rules, while Sergei playfully bent them. He continually tried the patience of their new coach, Vladimir Zaharov. Coach Zaharov put 14-year-old Sergei on a strict weight lifting program to build the muscles in his upper body. The two also had to relearn everything they had been doing as singles skaters. They had to align their bodies and skate in unison. This was an especially hard task for Sergei, who had to shorten his skating stride to match tiny Katia's. "His strokes were always shorter than was natural," Katia remembered.

The two spent hours on the ice learning jumps, spirals, lifts, and throws. From the start, Katia felt safe in her partner's arms during the lifts, but she became terrified of the throws. Katia got black and blue while trying to land after Sergei propelled her across the ice. "[T]he girl flies much higher than when she jumps alone. She travels farther in the

They Died Too Young

air," Katia explained. After many throws, Sergei would say to his partner, "Don't you think you should go unlace your skates for a while? Go sit a little bit. I can't throw you anymore." But Katia was determined to conquer her fear—and land the throws. As they continued, Sergei would make sad faces at Katia. "But he never got mad at me," Katia said. "Some partners got angry and screamed when the girls didn't land the throws. Pairs skating can be very, very dangerous for girls. I've seen boys, exasperated to the point of cruelty, purposely throw their partners in a different direction than she expects, or throw her too high on purpose. This can be deadly. But Sergei was never like this."

With their good work ethic and concern for each other, the new team of Gordeeva and Grinkov was beginning to learn the art of pairs skating.

Gordeeva and Grinkov perform their free skating program
en route to the gold medal at the World Figure Skating
Championships, Cincinnati, March 1987.

PARTNERS ON THE ICE

The pairing of fun-loving Sergei and serious-minded Katia was the right combination. Their personalities seemed to balance each other. Katia was proud that she was Sergei's partner, and Sergei, in turn, developed a brotherly affection for the young skater. Their skating was also progressing, and Coach Zaharov planned for them to start competing in junior competitions.

But the coach changed his mind after Sergei missed a morning practice early in the second year of training. Instead, he decided that Katia needed a new partner. Sergei's absence was one too many and convinced Zaharov that Sergei didn't have the discipline to become a champion. He sent Katia home and called both skaters' parents to come to the rink the next morning for a meeting. Instead of waiting until the next day, though, the Gordeevs and Grinkovs met to discuss Sergei's missing practice. When he learned about Zaharov's decision not to coach him anymore, Sergei called Katia. The two met at the subway the next morning to discuss their options.

At the meeting between the families, the skaters, and Zaharov, Katia and Sergei both knew they wanted to keep skating together. Luckily, their parents supported their decision, and the two got a new coach, Nadezheda Shevalovskaya. She introduced the pair to the person who was to have perhaps the most influence on the skating style of Gordeeva and Grinkov, choreographer Marina Zueva. Marina was a former ice dancer who was studying to get a degree in choreography from the National Theater Institute in Moscow. She created several early programs for the young pair, but more importantly, she taught them about movements and expressions. She helped them understand that there was more to a program than just the individual elements. "'How would you act out spring? Do flowers, birds, love, sun,'" Katia remembers Marina saying. "'Now show me winter. Or, make this shape for me on the ice.' Sergei would laugh sometimes at these exercises, because Marina used unusual words." With Marina's guidance, the young pair added new depth to their skating. The next step was international competition.

In December 1983 the pair traveled to Sapporo, Japan, for their first junior World Championships. The nervousness they felt showed in their skating, and they placed sixth. Frustrated, but relieved they'd completed their first big competition, 16-year-old Sergei and 12-year-old Katia returned home to the Soviet Union determined to win the event the next year.

With the help of a new coach, Stanislav Leonovich, and Marina, they did just that. The contest was held in Colorado Springs, Colorado, and the two were not expected to win. However, many skaters struggled with the high altitude of the mountainous city, finding it hard to catch their breath or complete their jumps. Sergei and Katia were one of the few pairs who skated a clean program. The result was a gold medal.

The 1984 junior Worlds not only marked the pair's first victory, it was also their first visit to the United States. It was December, and Katia remembers there was snow and "Christmas trees decorated with beautiful ornaments." Sergei and Katia took walks together and went shopping for gifts and souvenirs. Many skaters teased Sergei that his little partner had a crush on him, but he never got too upset. Instead, his head was turned by some of the ice dancers, girls closer to his age. He regarded Katia with affection, but never thought of her as a potential girlfriend.

Meanwhile, Katia's crush on her partner was deepening, but she kept her feelings to herself. On Sergei's 18th birth-

They Died Too Young

day, she gave him his first gift. "It was a key chain that my father had brought back from Spain. It had a little gun on it that could shoot caps, and although this was a small gift, I was so shy that I worried about it endlessly. But Sergei liked it and kept it with him, which made me happy," she wrote in *My Sergei*. He, in turn, gave her a gift for her 14th birthday in May. Sergei called Katia and asked her to meet him near the subway station. It was rare for the two to spend much time together off the ice, so Katia excitedly ran to find Sergei holding a huge brown-and-white stuffed dog.

Not long after they exchanged gifts, it was time to begin learning their routines for the new skating season. Marina created a challenging short program of piano ragtime music for the pair, which involved a lot of fancy footwork and pantomime. Sergei enjoyed the program and was a natural at picking up the meaning as well as the individual elements of the piece. He worked with Katia on the short and long programs, set to a medley of big band music. Despite their hard work, Katia fell on the side-by-side triple Salchow in the artistic program in the Skate Canada event. This difficult jump requires the skater to take off from a back inside edge of one blade and complete three revolutions before landing on the back outside edge of the other skate. The fall was disappointing, but the result was disastrous.

Stanislav Zhuk, the strict head of the army club, saw Katia's fall and blamed the mistake on a bad program. He believed that there was too much choreography in the routine, and that skaters should only concentrate on the required elements. He saw promise in the pair and decided to coach them himself. "Thus began the longest year of skating that Sergei and I ever endured," Katia wrote in her memoirs.

Eighteen-year-old Sergei immediately disliked Zhuk and disagreed with his teaching methods. Zhuk was a former European pairs champion who drank too much and used profanity around his students. He allegedly even tried to seduce some of the older, more mature female skaters.

Sergei hated Zhuk's behavior and even boldly stood up to him on some occasions.

Sergei had graduated from high school, and since he no longer attended class, he liked to nap for a few hours between the morning and evening practices. Zhuk claimed that any nap over 45 minutes made a skater too relaxed for the evening practice. He began telling people that Sergei was lazy and undisciplined. He also told Katia she should get a new partner. Katia, however, was more sure than ever that she and Sergei should continue skating together. Sergei just had his own "code for living," Katia said. "Even though he never told anybody this code, he always lived by it. Sergei knew what was right and what wasn't." This unspoken confidence was one of the things that Katia most admired in her partner.

Consequently, Sergei would ignore Zhuk when he was off the ice. "Sergei used to say to Zhuk, 'After practice, what I want to do is none of your business. If I want a beer, I'll have one. If it's Saturday and we don't skate, I won't get up at 7:00 A.M.,'" Katia recalled.

It was a rare Saturday, though, that the pair wasn't practicing. Zhuk believed in hard training. When they weren't on the ice, he had them running, weight lifting, throwing rocks, and snorkeling to help control their breathing. Zhuk also tried to separate Katia and Sergei off the ice, but they only became better friends. The two bonded even more to get through their time with the "miserable, pitiless Zhuk," as they called him.

For the pair's first senior-level competition, the 1986 Soviet Nationals, Sergei and Katia were overtrained and mechanical. Still, they finished second to the defending champions, Elena Valova and Oleg Vassiliev. The pair also placed second at the European Championships in Copenhagen. By the time the World Championships arrived, Sergei and Katia realized they needed a new coach. But after they won the event held in Geneva, Switzerland, they knew it would take some convincing for CSKA officials to let them change. After all, Gordeeva and Grinkov were world champions under Zhuk.

After their win, Sergei, Katia, and other champions went on a 20-city tour through Switzerland, France, and Germany, sponsored by the International Skating Union (ISU). What was supposed to be a moment of light-hearted glory for the pair was again ruined by Zhuk. He roomed with Sergei and followed him everywhere, not even allowing the Russian skaters to go out with others to the area attractions. One day Sergei, Russian skater Alexander (Sasha) Fadeev, and American champion Brian Boitano were able to break away from Zhuk, and they went for a walk. Boitano asked Fadeev, who spoke both Russian and English, to ask Sergei what he loved most about skating. His response startled the young American. "Sergei said that he didn't love skating. He skated because he had to," Katia remembered.

While his attitude toward skating eventually became more joyful again, Sergei was miserable that year of his first World Championship win. He also knew that if he wanted to continue skating, a change needed to be made. Sergei, Sasha, Marina, and fellow skater Anna Kondrashova drafted a letter to CSKA asking that Zhuk be removed as head coach. At their insistence, Katia also agreed to sign the letter. Soon, Stanislav Leonovich was once again reinstated as the pair's coach.

Skating became fun again. Marina created inventive new routines and Sergei discovered that even training wasn't so bad. When he missed a practice, Stanislav wouldn't yell, but instead remind him that because of his absence, they had more to work on. "There is more than just you, Sergei, who's involved," Leonovich would say. Sergei stopped missing practices and recommitted himself to the sport. The results were wins at the 1987 Soviet Nationals and World Championships.

Once again, the pair was asked to join a tour. This time, however, it was the chance to travel through America—and without Zhuk. Promoter Tom Collins invited the pair to visit 25 cities with his ensemble of skaters. Although they didn't speak English, Katia and Sergei agreed. They were spending more and more time together off the ice, and Sergei was noticing his partner in a new way. He would hug her, hold her hand sometimes, or casually put his arm around her. "I figured it was only because he was excited to be on this tour and was feeling so good that he did it," Katia wrote in *My Sergei.* "I didn't think it had anything to do with me." But very slowly Sergei was falling in love with his partner.

All of his growing romantic feelings had to be put on hold, though, when they returned home to the Soviet Union. It was now an Olympic training year, and the pair had to buckle down for some hard work in preparation for the 1988 winter Olympic Games in Calgary, Alberta, in Canada. They spent much of the summer of 1987 traveling to training camps, practicing their new routines. The short program was set to the music of "The March of the Toreadors" from the opera *Carmen,* while the long program was a medley of piano pieces by Mendelssohn, Chopin, and Mozart.

Life was busy, but the pair was feeling strong and confident, until mid-November. That's when Sergei's skate caught a soft rut in the ice and Katia, who was in a star lift, with her arms and legs fully extended high in the air above Sergei's head, fell to the ice forehead first. Katia was hospitalized for six days, and Sergei visited her almost every day, even bringing a bouquet of roses on his first visit. Katia was upset with her partner at first. "But Sergei was so sad that I began to feel sorry for him. He stayed in the hall after giving me the roses, and it scared him when they wheeled me out of the room in my bed so I could go have some tests." After being hospitalized, Katia stayed home for a week of rest, and again, Sergei visited her every day. Once they were allowed back on the ice, Sergei held onto his partner more tightly than ever before. "Something had happened in those two weeks, and even I . . . realized that his thoughts for me had changed. Before we had been like two skaters. After that, we were a pair," Katia explained.

Their newfound connection helped them win the European Championships, their last big event before the Olympic Games.

Sergei and Katia skate at the Calgary Olympics,
February 1988.

PARTNERS IN LIFE

Sergei celebrated Christmas 1987 with Katia and her family. The outgoing young man was surprisingly shy around the Gordeevs, but Katia did her best to make him feel welcome at their celebration. He even took part in the family's new-found tradition of breaking a plate on the floor, making a wish on a broken piece, and hiding that piece somewhere in the apartment. Katia wished the pair would skate well in Calgary, but she never found out what Sergei had wished for that night.

Before they had the chance to settle in at the Olympic village, Sergei turned 21. Katia gave him a charm of the Olympic symbol, which he added to a chain he wore around his neck. It had been an intense year for the pair, and Sergei felt closer than ever to his partner. But he was unable to practice for two days when he came down with a case of the stomach flu. He couldn't eat for three days. Meanwhile, Katia was scared Sergei wouldn't get well. She spent much of her time in the cafeteria eating cheesecake to calm her nerves.

Still, the pair managed to be ready for their short program, in which they placed first. After their artistic program, Ekaterina Gordeeva and Sergei Grinkov became the latest in a long line of pairs skaters to become gold medalists at the Olympics. Every judge scored them first. "Gordeeva and Grinkov were head over heels over the rest of them," U.S. pairs coach Ron Ludington said. "They were so beautiful in unison when they did their spins and jumps that you didn't notice the difference in their size," choreographer and former pairs champion Sandra Bezic told *Sports Illustrated*.

The world had fallen in love with tiny Katia and the rugged Sergei. They became celebrities in the media. Immediately, debate began about whether the two were romantically involved. Some said they skated like brother and sister, while others, like sportswriter E. M. Swift, saw Sergei as the older brother's friend "who suddenly realizes that the little girl with whom he is dancing has grown into a woman."

Off the ice, however, Sergei was still unsure how to act around Katia. They had held hands and even hugged, but they had never kissed. The age difference also made it hard for them to spend much time together. Sergei celebrated their Olympic win with friends, hitting the nightclubs in Calgary, while Katia stayed in her room and wrote in her journal. When they were together during this time, it was usually for an interview. When asked how long the pair planned to skate together, Sergei replied, through an interpreter, "We will skate as long as we're still young." He also told the press that he didn't have time for a girlfriend. But Victor Rhyzkin, a coach at the figure skating club, revealed, "The girls like him better than ice cream." When asked if Katia minded these attentions, he replied, "On the inside she probably suffers. But she doesn't show it. Anyway, it is not good for a romantic relationship between pairs skaters. They start to argue all the time." But before the year was over, Sergei and Katia were decidedly in love.

In the months following their Olympic win, Katia matured, growing two inches and gaining five pounds, but she also grew confused about where she stood with Sergei. While they spent a lot of time alone together off the ice, Sergei rarely asked Katia to join him when he went out with friends. Perhaps he was also trying to figure out where their relationship was heading. His indecision hurt Katia, but the two never spoke about their feelings. Still, Sergei gave Katia good advice and spoke to her like a friend. One time when Katia was having self-doubts, he told her he liked her just the way she was. He even gave her advice on how to deal with failure and disappointment: "If you're disappointed with yourself, don't show it to people. You have to have the strength to handle it." His words of advice made Katia idolize him all the more for his confidence and maturity. When she suffered a stress fracture in her foot in the fall of 1988 and couldn't practice, Sergei lifted her in his arms and skated her around the ice.

As the year of triumph and disappointment (they had lost their first World Championship in three years) came to a close, Sergei made plans to spend New Year's Eve with his friend Sasha, turning down Katia's invitation to visit a family friend's dacha (vacation home). Instead, she gave him a bottle of sweet liqueur as a gift and wished him a happy New Year. But that night, on the way to visit Sasha's new sauna in the country, Sergei decided to visit Katia to see if she wanted to come too. The small house was within walking distance of where Katia was staying, so she joined them on the cold trek through the snow to the cabin. But only Sasha opted for a sauna that night. Instead, Sergei and Katia shared their first kiss. Soon after, each revealed their romantic feelings for the other.

Appropriately, their first competition as a couple was held in the romantic city of Paris, France. Even though they had told only one person—Sergei's sister, Natalia—that they had fallen in love, everyone who saw them stroll around the city could tell that they were young lovers. For the first time, they paid more attention to each other both on and off the ice than they did to their skating. Their feelings, however, translated into their performances, and they won their third World Championship.

For the first time in the nearly eight years they had known each other, Sergei started telling Katia his hopes and dreams for the future. He loved reading about different cultures and wanted to travel all over the world. He also wanted to learn how to speak English. But first, Sergei wanted to own a car and move into an apartment. Although the Soviet

Union had promised him both of these things, months had gone by and he was still waiting. When the 22-year-old threatened to quit skating, he soon received a car and was promised an apartment within the next year. The two traveled all over the Russian countryside together in Sergei's new car. They even joked that if Sergei never got his own apartment, they might live in the car one day and raise their family.

Meanwhile, on the ice, Marina Zueva created routines that fit the pair's mood of blossoming romance and love. The music of Tchaikovsky's *Romeo and Juliet* became the backdrop for one of the most memorable routines of Gordeeva and Grinkov. The pair used it to win the 1990 European and World Championships. Although the program was beautiful, one of its moves—the loop lift—was very painful for Sergei. Despite the fact that Katia was only 95 pounds, lifting her with just one hand over the years had caused Sergei to have some shoulder problems. Sergei tried not to complain about the pain, but he needed shots to ease his discomfort. Later, doctors in the United States realized that he had been skating with a torn rotator cuff (the group of muscles that controls shoulder rotation) for over a year.

But that pain inflicted by his injury was small compared to the news Sergei received in the spring of 1990. While the pair was on a U.S. tour, he learned that his father, who was 56, had died of a heart attack. He cried when he learned the news and was sad that he hadn't spent enough time with him. Mikhail Grinkov had suffered three heart attacks before the one that took his life; he died in his wife's arms. When Sergei returned from the funeral in Moscow, he told Katia, "Every year it's something. First my best friend [died]. Then Moshka [Sergei's dog]. Then my father."

After the tragedy, Sergei received the deed to a studio apartment in Moscow. He had decided it was time to move on. On their first visit to see the apartment, 23-year-old Sergei proposed to 19-year-old Katia. "It wasn't the way

They Died Too Young

Sergei and Katia perform at an international free skating
competition in Kobe, Japan, in 1989.

Americans propose to a woman. He didn't invite me to dinner. He didn't give me a ring. He didn't get on his knees and ask me to marry him," she revealed in her book. "Sergei just said, 'I would love for you to live with me in this apartment.'" To commemorate the occasion, Sergei later bought his bride-to-be a delicate antique emerald ring with small diamonds in the setting. The couple filed their marriage license and were officially married on April 20, 1991. Eight days later, they had a church ceremony and reception for family and friends. As a wedding gift, Katia's mother renovated Sergei's studio apartment. The newlyweds now had their first home.

With the big changes in their personal life, the pair also made a big jump in their professional lives as well. They left the amateur ranks and turned professional, signing with International Management Group (IMG). Suddenly they were allowed to make their own schedules and decisions about everything, from when to practice to what to eat. The freedom was overwhelming at first, but also liberating. The decision turned out to be the right one for the pair. They competed in their first professional event, the World Professional Championships, in December 1990, and came in second place. Exactly one year later, they won the event.

The summer after Katia and Sergei married, they toured with the Tom Collins show and then went on another tour to South Africa. The busy couple saw this time as a honeymoon. They agreed to join another tour, Stars on Ice, and they skated with the group for the next three consecutive seasons.

While on tour with Stars on Ice at the beginning of 1992, Katia began to feel strange. She was tired and temporarily lost her sense of smell. She found out she was pregnant. Katia was scared—she didn't want to miss a whole year of skating. She also didn't know how to tell Sergei. They had never talked about having children, and she wasn't sure how

They Died Too Young

he would react to the news. After he stayed out late one night with friends, she blurted out the news in anger. Sergei, however, was thrilled at the thought of becoming a father. After some discussion, they decided to finish out the tour (which ended in April). Katia was due to deliver on September 20.

But Daria Sergeyevna Grinkova arrived nine days early, on September 11, 1992. In just three years, Sergei and Katia had gone from skating partners to proud new parents.

Sergei and Katia perform in the pairs figure skating
competition at the 1990 Goodwill Games at the
Tacoma Dome in Tacoma, Washington.

LIFE IN AMERICA

As with most new parents, Sergei and Katia found their priorities changed after Daria's birth. They were excited, scared, and confused. When Katia was delivering Daria, Sergei followed Russian custom and did not stay with his wife in the hospital in Princeton, New Jersey. Instead, he was outside waiting in the car when a nurse came out to tell him he was needed inside. From the moment he saw five-pound, four-ounce Daria, Sergei's life was changed. He drank champagne to celebrate and then called everyone he knew with the good news. Sergei believed Daria was going to be a tennis player, since she was born the night after he and Katia got back from watching matches at the U.S. Open.

The next day, he brought Katia flowers and gifts. Finally, after three long days, Katia and Daria came home to the condominium near Princeton. Sergei was the happiest he had ever been. The young family welcomed the help of Elena Gordeeva. She came to stay with them and showed them how to burp, bathe, change, and care for their new daughter. Every morning Sergei woke up anxious to see Daria, knowing that each day would bring something new. He also knew that he and Katia would have to get back in shape if they wanted to keep skating with Stars on Ice, which was to begin rehearsals in just one month.

Soon Katia was back in the gym and on the ice, getting back her jumps. There were a few falls, but overall Katia and Sergei were pleased with their progress and excited to skate again. The only problem facing them was what to do with little Daria. Life on the road was hard enough for just the two of them, but it was impossible with a baby. They didn't want to leave Daria with strangers either, but they needed to make money to support their family. Finally, Elena volunteered to take care of the infant. "You're young, and you love your work," she told the couple. "Better that you should miss Daria than she has to follow you around the country living in hotels."

The decision was the hardest the couple had ever faced, but they left Daria, whom they had nicknamed Dasha, with Elena and traveled to Lake Placid for rehearsals. Being apart from Daria was torture, but they believed they had made the right choice. The skating community welcomed them back with open arms, and the new parents proved they were still champions, winning the World Professional Figure Skating Championships in December.

Sergei felt they needed a home base in America. On impulse, the young family bought a house in Tampa, Florida. Only later did they realize it had been a mistake. They hardly spent any time there, and in 1994 they left the house for a condominium in Simsbury, Connecticut. The condo was just minutes from the International Skating Center, a new state-of-the-art training facility. Many other skaters, including singles skaters Oksana Baiul and Viktor Petrenko, also moved into the complex.

The couple was happy that Elena and Daria now had a place to stay in America. The Soviet Union had seen the fall of Communism just a few years earlier, in 1991, and the country was being torn apart internally. There were refugees in the streets and mafia groups demanding payment from new business owners. While many saw the collapse of Communism as good for the former Soviet Union in the long run, people were suffering from its immediate effects. Sergei was especially troubled by what was happening. Prices for goods were skyrocketing and his mother was on a fixed income. While he liked America and all the opportunities it afforded him, he was "Russian to his soul," Katia wrote, "and was only comfortable there." She explained, "He came to

They Died Too Young

Sergei lifts Katia during their gold medal pairs performance at the 1994 winter Olympics in Hamar, Norway.

America to work, and he returned to Russia to find peace of mind. He thought the fundamental difference between Americans and Russians was that the Russian culture was so rich, so old, that the people had a very deeply rooted mentality. There was a stolidness, a steadfastness, a stoicism, and a respect for tradition that was uniquely Russian." Sergei was grateful for the opportunity to live in both countries. He also liked the fact that Daria was a dual citizen of both the United States and Russia. Upon turning 18, she could choose to which country she wanted to belong.

After their second Olympic win, Sergei and Katia took some time off to enjoy their new home and spend time with Daria, who was by then almost two years old. Sergei and Katia set to work decorating their new home. Sergei wallpapered a room for Daria, set up her crib, and hung pictures and a mirror. The room was a surprise to both his wife and his little daughter.

In the summer of 1994 they started working with Marina on their new routines. One new program, which they dubbed "the Rodin number," was set to the music of Rachmaninoff. The program required the pair to imitate the poses of sculptures by the famous French artist Auguste Rodin. "Sergei's body was like a Greek god's. And her body is just like a sculpture," Marina explained of her choices. "You can't add anything to them. You just take what they have and fix [the moment]. This moment, how people love each other, is perfect. I wanted to fix this moment for Sergei and Katia forever, how they love each other." It quickly became one of Katia's favorites. The pair used it to win their fourth World Pro Championships.

Soon it was time for another year with Stars on Ice. This time there were four other Russians in the cast—pairs team Elena Bechke and Denis Petrov and ice dancers Natalia Annenko and Genrikh Sretenski. They could speak and joke in Russian, but also tried to participate in conversations with the rest of the cast. Sergei was now opening up more to his new family at Stars on Ice, and the cast noticed the change. "As Grinkov learned more English, and after Daria's birth, his face during performances became more open; the warm soul shone through, so that audiences could see what his close friends saw every day," wrote skating expert Beverley Smith in her book *A Year in Figure Skating.* "The better his English got, the bigger his personality got," said Canadian skater Kurt Browning. "In the beginning, you would just get a nod from him," skater Brian Orser explained. "Then it got to 'Hello, Brian,' in his accent. He would chuckle trying to say that."

Still, the language barrier didn't prevent Sergei from having a close friendship with American skater Scott Hamilton. The friends even developed a skit for Stars, in which Scott dances around the ice with Katia while Sergei watches intently, jealousy in his eyes. Then later on, when Scott tries to repeat the move, Sergei would tap him on the shoulder. "I brush him off, like 'Don't bother me, I'm busy,'" Hamilton said. "And he hits me harder. I turn around to look, and my nose goes into his chest and I realize I'm up against something a little more powerful than what I want to deal with, and I tiptoe away," the 5-foot 3-inch skater revealed. Sergei may have had trouble speaking English, but he understood it pretty well. He often explained Scott's jokes to Katia in Russian. "When you look at Sergei's presence and his physical size, it's deceiving, because there was a gentleness and always a wonderful sense of humor and an instant ability to laugh," Scott remembered. Their senses of humor were often at battle as each was constantly playing jokes, trying to one-up the other. "I'd get him three or four times a day," Scott revealed. "He'd look at me sometimes as if to say, 'What are you going to do next?'" Other skaters enjoyed Sergei's laugh and his mischievous behavior. "He took his skating very seriously, but he didn't take himself seriously," tour choreographer Sandra Bezic remembered.

Sergei loved traveling and meeting fans, but he disliked the receptions after the show, where he was expected to

Olympic skater Scott Hamilton joins Sergei to listen to
the warm-up music before practice for a Stars on Ice
production in Lake Placid, New York.

mingle with the press and other people the tour's promoters deemed important. Instead, he had a knack for remembering the "little" people at the different arenas from year to year. He'd say hello to the zamboni drivers, dressing room attendants, security guards, and fans he remembered from the year before. "Sergei was the absolute opposite of a snob," Katia recalled. "In fact, I think he'd have preferred to spend an evening with these people than in the company, even, of skaters."

Eventually, Sergei's English improved and he surprised people with his newfound vocabulary. "He was coming to the rink and saying, 'Good morning, Kurt. And how are you?'" Kurt Browning recalled. And I'd say, 'Oh hi, Sergei. I'm good. And you?' He'd always say, 'Oh, I'm not too bad.' We [members of the tour] didn't really realize all [his] little Sergei-isms until we all started saying them to each other. When we'd want to remember him we'd all say, 'Ab-so-lute-ly!' It was his favorite word." It was a word Sergei used frequently, especially in response to the free meals served to them while practicing at the rink. "We were on the tour for 50 dates together, with catering at the rink, and Scott would say to him every other show, 'Ready for free food, Sergei?' He'd reply, 'Ab-so-LUTE-ly.'"

Eating and having fun were two of Sergei's favorite activities. "Quite often on tour, when you wanted to go for dinner, they were one of the first to call," remembers Brian Orser. "He didn't like turkey, but he liked sushi, and so did Katia. He'd eat his, and finish hers, too."

Most of all, Sergei loved Katia and Daria. The other skaters, most of whom did not have children, also loved visits from the rambunctious toddler. They dubbed them "Dasha days." On the day of Sergei's death, November 20, 1995, Scott shouted out to Sergei, "Tomorrow is a Dasha day!" Proud father Sergei threw his jubilant arms in the air at the news. But he never saw his beloved Dasha again.

Katia hugs her daughter, Daria, after her skating routine
at a tribute to her husband and Daria's father,
Sergei Grinkov.

TRAGEDY ON THE ICE

In the years before his death, Sergei visited many doctors. He had surgeries on his shoulder and was given complete physicals before major competitions, but no doctor ever found anything wrong with the young man. He seemed to be the picture of health.

His life was also blessed. In April 1995 Sergei and Katia traveled back to Simsbury to spend time relaxing at home. Every morning they sat on the porch and had breakfast. Sergei fed the squirrels, and they watched Daria. At the end of May, Sergei drove his wife to New York City and bought her a Louis Vuitton handbag. The next morning he made her breakfast in bed. Katia had told castmates of Stars that she wished Sergei would surprise her with breakfast in bed. Sergei usually never surprised Katia with gifts; he needed her help in picking them out. He also didn't know how to cook. But after watching his wife work the coffee maker, he decided to surprise her on her birthday. He added toast, orange juice, and a bouquet of fresh flowers to the tray he handed to an astonished Katia.

With summer upon them, it was time to start skating again. This season, however, Sergei was having trouble with his back. He saw a variety of doctors in both the United States and Russia, but nothing seemed to ease his pain. Some days the 28-year-old even had trouble walking. Instead of skating, he swam, lifted weights, and did special exercises. Sergei also spent lots of time with Daria. "Every afternoon Sergei took Daria for a walk and played with her outside. He was such a good father. He'd become so strong, not only with his muscles, but as a person. More of a father. More of a husband. I felt so proud of him that summer," Katia remembered.

41

While he never felt completely pain-free on the ice again, Sergei was well enough to get back to skating again. The pair had decided to forget about competitions and instead look ahead to the 55-city Stars on Ice tour. That fall they rented a condo in Lake Placid, where Daria and Katia's parents joined them. Marina also visited to help them with their new program.

On November 20, Marina, Sergei, and Katia were working on the finishing touches of the program. They decided to run it through from the beginning. Early on in the program, Sergei's hands didn't go around Katia's waist for a lift. He bent over and tried to catch his breath. He was dizzy, and Katia knew that something was wrong. Very carefully, Sergei lay down on the ice. He had stopped breathing and couldn't speak. He could not answer all the questions Katia and Marina were asking. Marina knew it was a problem with Sergei's heart. She made Katia run and call 911, and she administered CPR until medical technicians arrived. But it was too late. Two-time Olympic, four-time world champion, husband, and father Sergei Grinkov was dead.

At the hospital, after Sergei was pronounced dead, Katia unlaced his skates. She now had to deal with the fact that he would never wear them again. The world was shocked, and the skating community mourned the death of someone so young and talented. Everyone wanted to know what went wrong.

"He was dead the moment he hit the ice—he felt no pain," Dr. Josh Schwartzberg, the doctor who worked for over an hour trying to revive Sergei, told *People* magazine. Doctors performed an autopsy to figure out what had happened to Sergei. His heart was enlarged, a trait that is not unusual in world-class athletes. However, Sergei's enlargement may have been caused by high blood pressure. Additionally, the left artery of his heart was almost completely blocked. This blockage had caused Sergei's massive heart attack. Doctors reported that he may have suffered a "silent" heart attack within the previous 24 hours but might have attributed any pain to the problems that plagued his

They Died Too Young

back and shoulder. "He was clearly in very good health except for this one problem," said Dr. Francis Varga, the doctor who performed the initial autopsy. "The entire front half of his heart muscle and a part of the left side of his heart muscle were deprived of oxygen. If he continued at all on any schedule, it was only a question of time. Unless his condition was discovered and he had a bypass, the probability of survival for him was remote. Many times in young people the first sign of coronary artery disease is sudden death."

Through a blood sample received six months after Sergei's death, doctors at Johns Hopkins University discovered that the skater had carried a defective gene that contributes to heart disease. Up to 20 percent of the world's population may carry this gene, which they named, "the Grinkov risk."

The discovery was little consolation to 24-year-old Katia, who was now a widow and single mother. Her family and friends had always seen the petite woman as fragile, but Katia surprised them with her strength and resolution. She decided that Sergei, with his Russian soul, should be buried in Moscow. Skating friends first got the chance to say goodbye to their friend at a wake in Saranac Lake, New York. Katia wore Sergei's wedding ring on a chain around her neck. "It was too perfect, maybe. It's only fairy tales that have happy endings," she told Scott Hamilton. "Everything was too good with me and Sergei for it to end happily." Five days after his death, Sergei was laid to rest at Vaganosky Cemetery in Moscow, a resting place for many famous Russians. Nearly 12,000 people attended his funeral.

Afterward, Katia followed the traditional Russian custom of mourning for 40 days. People assumed she would never skate again. Katia, however, wanted to honor Sergei. On February 27, 1996, she did just that in a tribute called "A Celebration of a Life." Some of the biggest names in skating gathered in Hartford, Connecticut, to skate in a show dedicated to Sergei's memory. After months of struggling with her grief and depression, Katia took to the ice in front of an audi-

Olympic skaters Scott Hamilton and Paul Wylie (right) pay their last respects to Sergei Grinkov during a farewell ceremony.

ence again. But this time she was alone. The routine she skated depicted her life with Sergei and the tragedy she had endured. After her flawless performance that brought the audience to its feet in tears, Katia addressed the crowd. "Try to find happiness in every day. At least once, smile to each other every day. And say just one extra time that you love the person who lives with you. Just say, 'I love you.'"

Katia had another way to let Sergei know, even in death, that she would never forget him. She collaborated with sportswriter E. M. Swift to write a memoir, which she titled *My Sergei: A Love Story*. When it was released in the fall of 1996, the book quickly rose to the top of the *New York Times* bestseller list. It was then made into a television movie, which aired on February 4, 1998, the day that would have been Sergei's 31st birthday. "I dedicate this book to my Seriozha. To my lover, my husband, the father of my child, a great sportsman, and my best friend," she wrote in Russian in the book's introduction. "During his short and intense life Sergei managed to give to many people some minutes of

They Died Too Young

Katia (right), Sergei's sister, Natalia (center), and Sergei's mother, Anna, (left) honor Sergei at the farewell ceremony in Moscow, November 25, 1995.

beauty. He lived for love and could give it to people because love was his natural state. I am grateful to Seriozha for every day I lived at his side, for every smile, every kind word. Seriozha, I'll treasure our wonderful fairy tale which we both lived and I'll tell it to our daughter."

Young Daria helped keep Katia going following Sergei's death, and today she serves as a reminder of his presence. Her bright blue eyes and wide smile are Sergei's, as is her energy and mischievous spirit. "We talk about Sergei a lot. She knows everything about her father and what role he plays in her life—he always will play a big role. He was half of my life . . . he's always here. I don't know what else to say. I feel like he's always there, around."

In the fall of 1996 Katia decided she would make a career as a singles skater, and today she continues to tour with Stars on Ice. "I worried so much that my skating will not be that beautiful without Sergei and that I will never bring people joy like we did together. I thought going back on the ice would

Ekaterina finishes her skating tribute, "A Celebration of a Life" for Sergei.

be a selfish thing to do without him. But I need my skating. It's treatment for me." Because of her strength and appeal, Katia landed an endorsement deal with Target stores. She now has two perfumes that bear her name and a doll made in her likeness. She also appeared in print ads for Rolex watches. (Sergei gave Katia a Rolex after Daria was born, which she still wears today.)

Despite all of her success and her busy schedule, Katia still works to honor her late husband's memory. In the spring of 1999 she helped raise money to create Sergei's Garden at Target House in Memphis, Tennessee. The house offers a home away from home for sick children and their families. It's the kind of place to which a man who loved children so much would be proud to lend his name.

"First of all, he was a man. Then he was a skater," Katia said. That is how the world remembers Sergei Grinkov.

Sergei Grinkov

They Died Too Young

Further Reading

Gordeeva, Ekaterina, with Antonina W. Bouis. *A Letter for Daria*. Boston: Little, Brown, and Company, 1998.

Gordeeva, Ekaterina, with E. M. Swift. *My Sergei: A Love Story*. New York: Warner Books, 1996.

Hill, Anne E. *Ekaterina Gordeeva*. Philadelphia: Chelsea House Publishers, 1999.

Popescu, Julian. *Russia*. Philadelphia: Chelsea House Publishers, 1998.

Shea, Pegi Deitz. *Ekaterina Gordeeva*. Philadelphia: Chelsea House Publishers, 1999.

Smith, Beverley. *A Year in Figure Skating*. Toronto: McClelland & Stewart, 1996.

Swift, E. M. "A Magical Twosome." *Sports Illustrated,* February, 29, 1988.

Chronology

1967	Sergei Mikhailovich Grinkov is born on February 4.
1972	Begins skating at the Central Red Army School (CSKA).
1981	Paired with 10-year-old Ekaterina Gordeeva.
1983	Sergei and Katia place sixth at the junior World Championships in Sapporo, Japan.
1984	Sergei and Katia win the junior World Championships in Colorado Springs.
1986	Grinkov and Gordeeva win the gold medal at the World Championships in Geneva.
1987	They win the World Championships in Cincinnati, Ohio.
1988	They win the gold medal at the Olympics in Calgary; Sergei and Katia share their first kiss on New Year's Eve.
1989	Grinkov and Gordeeva win their third World Championship title in Paris.
1990	The pair win their fourth World Championship, in Halifax, Nova Scotia, Canada; Sergei gets title to an apartment and proposes to Katia.
1991	Marries Katia on April 20; they begin touring with Stars on Ice.
1992	Daughter Daria Sergeyevna Grinkova is born on September 11.
1994	Grinkov and Gordeeva win the gold medal at the Olympic Games in Lillehammer.
1995	Sergei dies in Lake Placid on November 20.
1996	Katia skates in "A Celebration of a Life"; Grinkov and Gordeeva are inducted into the World Figure Skating Hall of Fame on May 12; *My Sergei* is published.
1998	Television version of *My Sergei* airs.
1999	Sergei's Garden at Target House opens.

INDEX